Shifting Shades of Sunlight

Other poetry books by
Mary Rogers-Grantham

It's Okay: Poetic Memoirs
Clear Velvet
Under a Daylight Moon
When the Sun Sails

Shifting Shades of Sunlight

New and Selected
Poetry and Prose

Mary Rogers-Grantham

CHM Media, Publisher

ISBN 979-8-9873184-2-3
Library of Congress Control Number: 2023937997

Published by CHB Media
(386) 492-6568
chbmedia@gmail.com
www.chbbooks.com

First Edition
Printed in the USA

ACKNOWLEDGMENTS

My gratitude to the following places for publishing these poems:

Cadence, Florida State Poets Association Anthology - "One Hundred and Thirty-Six," also a first-place winning poem in their annual contests.

Cadence, Florida State Poets Association Anthology, "Blue Mists"

The Florida Writer, "The Sky Was Missing a Star"

The Florida Writer, "For the Love of Mindfulness"

Cultural Daily, "No Guarantee"

The Isolation Challenge, Poets Look at the Covid 19 Pandemic "Rhythms," Marc Davidson, Editor

Of Poets and Poetry, "Coveting Hope"

Haikuniverse, A Haiku

The Kansas City Star, "Wanting" my first published poem in the selected poems from my first collection *It's Okay: A Poetic Memoirs.*

"Birthing Exodus," The Lady, 1966 Oil on Canvas, Artist Balcomb Greene, *Poetic Visions Anthology*

My poems owe tremendous gratitude to my poetry professors and workshop leaders for teaching me the colorful art of writing, for supporting my love for words and for reminding me to keep them fresh. My gratitude to everyone who offer encouraging affirmations that continue to inspire me as a writer and confirm our connection.

I hope you enjoy navigating the dawn of my work to current day in this book of new poems and selected ones from previously published *It's Okay: Poetic Memoirs, Clear Velvet* and *Under a Daylight Moon.*

My unconditional gratitude to Gary Broughman, my editor and publisher at CHB Media Publishing for the beautiful work they produce including my last collection, *When the Sun Sails,* which is available on Amazon as will my forthcoming poetry collection, *A Rainbow at Midnight.*

CONTENTS

I was a Little who wanted a lot and then wanted more. I inhaled the alphabet, so I filled pages of paper with the new letters, like wall papering my memory.

Every alphabet was on my Most Wanted list and like a detective, I went in search of their secrets and I discovered that every one of them echoed the language of light. I always felt encouraged by my parents. My search continues to this day.

Shifting Shades of Sunlight

for my parents

They glowed like a bonfire on storytelling night.
They were the tentacles preceding dawn,
the rouse before sunrise, the sails that
penetrated morning and the authors of poems
inside their daily language they didn't write down.
They were shifting shades of sunlight,
shadows in many midnights, the sassiness
of hope and the pride inside teardrops.
They were certain like the North Star,
the Big Dipper and ocean tidal waves.
They gave birth to mirrors, their wary children.
Now, their voices are the dainty silent blooms
that gently sway to the theme of the wind at the
head of each mound while they rest evermore.

Opening New Poems

One Hundred and Thirty-Six

I come from a place where time slowly
simmered like a fresh cut of lean roast beef
in an unforgiving oven. I come from a place
where the audacity of weekday mornings
strummed my nostrils awake with the
arrogant aroma of roasted coffee searching
for a hot country breakfast.

Where Saturday morning sleep tasted like
fluffy homemade biscuits smothered in farm
butter and wild berry jelly with a side of
skillet fried red potatoes. Where Sunday
morning sleep tasted like a pitcher of ice
cold sweet tea, a few freshly squeezed
lemon slices floating like toy boats in a tub
of water. Where poetry basked in dialect and
culture emerged during family mealtime,
showed up during prayer time, and grew
wild in fields along highways.

I come from a place where I picked wild
blackberries by the gallon, walked barefoot
with scorpions and scaled trees that dared
me to fall. I come from a place where hours
in the dog days of summer moved at the
pace of a charming garden snail - no hurry,
no appointments – just navigating its destination.

I come from a place where the pride of
one hundred and thirty-six peace abiding folks
loved the smell of their Arkansas mountains.

Crowning Miss Willie from Center Point

for my Sunday School teacher

When I remember you,
I remember the anatomy of your Sunday crowns,
the rhythm of their wide-brims making classy debuts
while accenting the symphony of your graceful stride,
the mimicking sound of your Sunday best high heels
like cadence and repetition of a call and response spiritual.

When I remember you,
I remember my prissy Sunday School teacher,
leading your growing littles through sobering lessons
intended to floss our daily living. You lived on the edge
of our lives in the pews, as we tried to understand
one preacher in three persons, baritone, tenor
and Louis Armstrong. You simplified our wonder.

When I remember you,
I remember one of your favorite rituals,
afternoon outings on your front porch
swinging back and forth while fanning and dabbing
stubborn sweat beads taunting you and the art
of your daybreak make-up perfection.
Dainty handkerchiefs. Arkansas charisma.
Center Point, that is.

When I remember you,
I remember a genial role model, devout disciple,
a handsome lady who did all things well
and settled for nothing less of your students,
of your community and even of your garden vegetables.
Sunday crowns. Sunday School teacher.
I never get dressed without you, without your inspiration.
Miss Willie. Arkansas unique. Center Point, that is.

Blue Mists

for my loving husband
SGM Johnnie R. Grantham

I plant Florida lilies in perennial honor of you.
When they finally bloom red and white,
I'll stand among them as an offering of blue.

Lately, rubbing my hands together
is the only thing that makes my blood purr,
then pool into red carnations in my dreams.

Sometimes, in my dreams,
I wake in towering slash pine treetops–
cuddling me before lifting me to you.

Sometimes, in my dreams,
I wake in a ridge of hills that rise
like warm mists embracing me.

Sometimes, in my dreams,
I see soft white flower petals floating
above the sea and hear their light flutters.

Sometimes, in my dreams,
I watch giant distinct mountain cliffs
changing into amoeba like appearances.

Sometimes, in my dreams
two figures float above a meadow,
lengthened faces in distress saying goodbye.

Sometimes, I awake soaked in your presence.
I wish I could stretch the nights far into
wherever you are and bring you home to me.

The Sky Was Missing a Star

for my loving husband

"New beginnings are often disguised as painful endings."
— Lao Tzu

When you left, you didn't pack anything.
You weren't sure where you were going.
So, I watched you leave. It was one
of those sacred acts we both took part in,
but only one of us witnessed. I signed onto
the watch for the love of loving.
You weathered menacing temperatures
symbolizing a devoted and tireless,
confident and proud Sergeant Major.
I wanted to change everything.
I wanted to return to ROTC summer camp.
I wanted to relive that week of gazes and answers.
I wanted to color our rainbows all over again.
I wanted to walk with you on snow covered trails.
I wanted to hear the ice crunch beneath our feet.
When you left, you didn't pack anything.
I stood in the doorway between panic and love
and released you to the soldiers in the sky,
You disappeared and so did I,
into my worst nightmare,
a world without you.

On Cue

for Linda Cole

One. Two.
One. Two. Three. Four.
The trio begins
as smooth as finished gemstones.
Each one as unique as a new moist morning
that summons you to join it for a while.
The jazz pianist teases you.
The upright bass guitarist induces you.
Ms. Jazz Vocalist glides into your ears
and enters your senses like your favorite beach martini—
unchained.

The pulse of Cue Note Billiards introduces a new heartbeat
a jazz pulse with distinguished fresh vocal flavors
steeped in harmony and laced with flawless fluency
and organic skillfulness from the lady songstress—
unchained.

Jazz Batons

inspired by jazz and photography exhibition, "From Ella to Coltrane"

From the soils where their voices are buried,
their spirit and the legend of their music continue
to speak precisely through courageous newcomers
patiently committed to jazzing their listeners.

They still labor at the onset of evenings
when street lights gaze through windows
and soft ceiling lights silhouette dinner guests

& the bold bright sound of trumpet urges
  the body to shape itself
& the drums tap the head into a smooth
  bounce that only it hears
& the piano with centuries of spirituality
  is rhapsody in praise.

You see, they left exclamation marks,
their batons, at the end of their finals.
Like syllables, the next group take them,
create bebop and swing side-by-side
language playlists & pass them on & on & on.

When you listen to the sounds of hardworking
jazz saxophonists, you can hear something fresh.
They coddle each breath and pamper each note
that preserves the one patent sound worthy
of adding their name to growing controversial
lists of best tenor & alto sax players of all time.

No Guarantee

No guarantee you'll live to finish your high school years.
Vulnerability keeps company with you every day.
No guarantee you'll pursue your dreams - career, family
and old age. They are menaces to privilege.
No guarantee you'll live after being stopped because
"You fit the description of ... ."
A common and useful echo for damnation.

No guarantee you'll wake up refreshed in the morning
after going to bed in your own home.
No guarantee you'll make your destination or your return,
because fear threatens hope with the dare to live.
No guarantee you'll reap any of the benefits of jogging,
living longer is one of them.

Every day is a new day, and every day is a black day
detrimental to black males, detrimental to black females.
Every day is injurious, when breath blown into a creation,
the beginning of a living soul is interrupted.
Every day, mothers pray their children return home
safely to her or home to their place of residence.

What it means to be an American rekindles the sounds
of yawning arguments. What are the results?
What it means to be black in America remembers
yesterday's grief. Why is grief our testament today?
What it means to be American is to be the prototype
with favor. Other folks need to hyphenate.

Muted Treasure

The earth cradles another mother's child
Muted treasure, muted target, no smile.
Bullets in the head, bullets in the back
Black bodies drop, then a siren attacks.

Telling pastorals surveying a recycled movement,
landscape of blood and blockade, of tears and torment.
Scent from the coffee shop just across the street,
and a bold scent of fear taunt a colony of defeat.

Here is a mother's treasure for dirt to consume
For the agony of silent words, for grieving wounds
For earth to drown, for tears to repeat and rewind.
Here is muted treasure and cruelly penalized.

Taste of a Ripe Morning. Coffee.

a triolet

Dawn moves like honey crowning a slice of toast.
I can taste a ripe morning unfurling with time.
It uncovers the earth as night becomes a ghost.
Dawn moves like honey crowning a slice of toast.
Moon turns white in daylight on the coast.
The aroma of fresh ground beans floats like rhyme
Dawn moves like honey crowning a slice of toast.
I can taste a ripe morning unfurling with time.

Stirring Her Bedscape Awake

for Mother

After eastern cottontails
finish their winter diet
of bush buds, tree bark,
twigs and woody shoots,

after frigid water dripping
from the roof top
no longer pause as icicle
pendants or pose like stalactites,

after the last cold snap,
the last frost
and the soil leaves no doubt
of readiness and surprise,

she carefully lifts a crisp
brown blanket,
each leaf, its own piece
of purpose and easy release.

She gently stirs her sleeping
bedscape awake
and waits for perennial scarves
of spring and signs of Four O'Clocks.

She patiently waits for bushy trumpet
shaped bouquets of solid
reds and pinks, yellows and whites
and bi-colors to join the family.

She loves spending quiet afternoons
   waiting for the arrival of
bees and butterflies and ruby-throat
hummingbirds, pollinators by day.

She often waits late evenings to watch
   the dramatic night flight
and the feeding forays of the moth
pollinator by night, the Carolina sphinx.

Evening dims the sight of these dashing
   dainty flower damsels, but their
light citrus scent soothes her nostrils
and soothes the nostrils of another night.

Rhythms

Effects of a Pandemic

"It was the best of times, it was the worst of times, it was the age of wisdom ..."

From *A Tale of Two Cities* by Charles Dickens

The front of the world pulls down a mask
like covering daylight, like covering sunlight.
Communication modifies common formulas
into reverie, a replica of octaves separating a state of being.

Visions of now collide, your truth, my truth,
memorizing memory, sketching splintered moments.
Close of day kindles a spark. The world rolls away
into cold water ruffles, into windswept places.

Wondrous travels and smiling venues pause and wait
like planets for discovery, like planets for exploration
languishing in towers of nightmares footnoting desolation
needing the sight of conquest, needing the scent of oxygen.

We lose something of every day, the architect
of everyday. Then, there's the fluster of loss,
the next to last, igniting what is taken for granted.
Sundown brings tomorrow like floating driftwood.

Apologies are daily mysteries outliving human names.
What can justify implicit observations?
What can gratify human wilderness?
The gospel of necessity populated by extras.

Time is the silent mirror reflecting hope, reflecting life,
reflecting death. Time is the camera capturing illegible scriptures
uttered by helpers, uttered by families, uttered by sufferers.
All, quarantined martyrs, using all they have to conquer death.

Barren ceremonies of remembrance, ritual, love.
Absent. Glass barriers separate human touch, breath
and warm kisses. Commemorative haunting celebrations
created on a balcony, a street, a road, a highway.

Humbling transforming memoirs. Like the cry of an insect
in a noiseless wind, estranged endurance renders change.
Mute days of the week glide by, struggling to stay awake.
A helpless white bird dies before breathing.

Rhythms of a virus.

For the Love of Mindfulness

I am in love with you, forest,
inviting me to explore your
resources and to love your wild.

I am in love with you, flowers,
blooming like stranded rapture
exhaling art into a path of grief.

I am in love with you, sun,
nature of all things, power of life
circle of energy, circle of survival.

I am in love with you, breeze,
floating gently like a feather
reaching for the next moment.

I am in love with you, March,
moving spent leaves that fall
in the cough of your wind.

I am in love with you, Moon,
sneaking quietly into night
like the fright of past curfew

I am in love with you, day,
poised like a vein in an atlas
like an unexplored metaphor.

Elegy to Different

"The things that make me different are the things that make me, me." – Piglet

who summons courage every day
before entering an uncertain world

where unsolicited judgment
is the dividend of biased labels

created to censor the state of being
who you are and to minimize it.

So many diverse voices echo
in a diverse world where some

seek to silence their rhythm.
Different isn't always easy,

but being different is precious
like time, always moving forward,

never stopping, never looking back.
The weight of different is a reflection

of the world where images form words
and words form mental language frames.

Different, a duplex for navigating space.
Different, a filter for navigating proud.

Different is amazing, like the rhythm
of sunflowers, sun shadows and sun showers.

It's a journey across humanity making history
in a Tour de People working tirelessly for inclusion

while summoning courage every day
before entering an uncertain world.

A Haiku

Withered beach goers
exit bruised water and sand.
So, the ocean breathes.

Poems from Clear Velvet

Morning Artist

aged in layers
her hands like marionettes
grip her victim
this arctic morning

the broom her companion
head
bowed to her task
she

sweeps the
parking spaces and
sidewalks//she is

is an old
woman whose
faced filled with
storylines// each

with its own
setting in
a

geography of
living //her life
buried somewhere
in her hollow
cheeks//narratives
go untold while
she
continues a task

she knows by
heart//the monotonous
gravelly
sweeping sounds

on sidewalks and
parking spaces
rarely does she look
up

as cars drive into the parking lot
to occupy her spaces//rarely
does she
notice the drivers who
exit their cars and
travel her sidewalks

she asks
nothing //this artist of my mornings
no one seems
to notice her//maybe
she doesn't
mind

I notice her and
bid her a
cheery

"Good Morning!"

Turkic Caravan Woman

An Ancient Chinese Sculpture

if there was a woman
whose skin was as gray as museum galleries
that now house and guard her   if

there was a woman
who straddled linen layered humps
and traveled with camel caravans   if there

was a woman
who wore a lofty hat
and one-piece body suit draped in a tunic   if there was

a woman
who strong-armed an ancient beast
while her hungry child fed at her breast   if there was a

woman
with the courage to navigate a slow-witted creature
over sweltering dust drifted plains—

There was a Turkic Caravan Woman.

In Drab Rooms with Medicine Johns

thoughts from a jogger and her right knee

Neurologists attempted to liberate me
with their wit before sliding inside
their tunnel piped with Bach's *Sarabande*
in A Major. The last request.

No soft saffron lighting to erase
my senses. I closed my eyes, then
dared the spirited harpsichord
to dull the pulse in the tunnel.

No warmed dusk scented oils
to anoint my body nor massage
my tension. I pretended the cold
lubricants made the jabs easier.

New Johns.
Drab rooms.
Hard cots.

I became a prostitute
in a pool of inquiries.

Dazed eyes.
Muffled whispers.
Throbbing pain.

One week.
Two weeks.
Three months.
One year.

I took charge of my anatomy,
walked out of my last drab room
and set myself free from cheerful
medicine Johns, and their strange
beds in colorless rooms.

Travel Swatches I-VI

after Audre Lorde

I

Bel-lah
I used to love our child's play laughter
that often found its way to the ears
of authority, just after pee had soaked
clear through my skirt.
We laughed hard,
and then we exhaled.

II

Shari
I heard your edgy blues
but got bored with the body politic
when deception defied confidence
my soul became restless
when your acts of allegiance
emanated sinister repression.

III

Haley
I admired your valor
to teach Black students.
I am sorry you exchanged
their academic needs
with your daughter stories.
They show up in college English
incompetent.

IV

Belinda
Restless, erotic spirit
I am sorry your insatiable river

crossed the state line,
rolled into smoke filled parlors,
barbershops and noonday blues rooms.
"Them that got..."

V
Jolene
rebel English teacher
extracted remarks from players like,
"She's a looker" and "Hey girl."
Your man had to be your age
 and boast "a hard back."
Prancing before your students and
strutting among your colleagues,
I watched you on both runways,
model Body Belligerent.

VI
Bonnie
I remember your Paul Laurence Dunbar
raspy recitations to your literature students.
In your baritone smoker's voice
you eloquently delivered "We Wear the Mask,"
then, your transition rendition in dialect
of "Po Lil' Lamb.
I admired your courageous
Angela Davis sermonettes.
I dreamed you were a Black Panther.

Elegy for Pearl

"For everything there is a season..." (Ecclesiastes 3:1)

Her memorial service was over. We walked
out of the church at four in the afternoon.
A light mist, a brilliant sun and mourners
embraced us —sobering reminders
of our loved one, whose voice
would no longer kindle the hearth

of our lives. Somber faced chauffeurs
stood by opened doors, invited the family
inside gleaming black limousines. We sat down,
stared and waited. The sleek black hearse
ahead of us would lead the cavalcade
of cars wearing beads of headlights.

We passed the school grounds, the fairgrounds,
and Yark-Ghary's car lot. We passed mom and pop
stores heaving the aroma of Southern Sunset coffee
out their doors and through their windows. We passed
black Angus grazing in fields littered with loose saffron
colored grass in dense pasture lands.

The only expression was the driver's eyes darting
about the rearview mirror from one family member
to the other. Just beyond Capp Murray Bend
the cemetery came into full view. Like a blue print
on a plot of earth, grave markers and headstones
in formation —a layout for loved ones.

I Laughed My Belly into Jell-O

I stood in the doorway.

The ceiling fan turned slowly beneath
the light bulb, sending shivering glows
around the room like the last embers
of a campfire.

I entered your room.

One butterscotch left in cellophane
lay on your dresser. I remembered
your high school acting debut
in the comedy, *The Devil's Funeral,*
while eating it. I laughed my belly
into Jell-O.

I closed the door behind me.

A faded orange overstuffed chair
sat next to the bed. I walked over
and sat in it. An 81/2 x 12 framed
caricature of you boasting a boisterous
grin defied my sigh. I heard you laugh.
I laughed my belly into Jell-O.

I got up from the overstuffed chair.

While walking the compass of your room,
I grinned back at the photo. Your presence
embraced me; your eyes dried my tears.
A box of tissues sat on top of the dresser.
I took one and then, left your room.

Through my tears,
I laughed my belly into Jell-O.

Mourning in Daydreams

She wants to

watch you check
her out from shoes to hair,
then hear you say,
You're looking real fine, today

see you sitting in your chocolate
corduroy chair, rocking
back and forth while reading
Jet magazine

inhale smooth Gevalia mingled
with zesty chittlin vapors
in your pine wood kitchen
on Thanksgiving morning

taste your southern deep-fried
chicken and succulent garlic
meatloaf that could shut down
any New Orleans kitchen

hear your tenor hum melt
into Johnnie Taylor's crooning
"Nothing's as Beautiful as You"
on the blues radio station.

She wants to laugh with you again,
until tears and bellies roll.

Precinct Improvisation

I walk out the backdoor thinking my two-year-old black Lab, Hannah,
is following me, but
she bolts ahead, mindless

of the scandalous white ground cover and the unforgiving snowfall. The yard

is bright, the flower bed is next to the weathered wooden fence,
the book on the
hearth is *A Christmas Carol.*
This morning I'm thinking of the laughter inside paucity at the Cratchit house

and I stare at Hannah like I'm looking through the night,

counting snowflakes.
She wants to pee, I can't
blame her for that,
and maybe a smile looks idiotic when it grows into a grin,

but she tells me
she loves this, she tells me she's not afraid.

She pees, she expects to play.

The snow-covered precinct. The white shawl houses.
Draw a circle in the snow with your foot. Imagine a hike in the Sedona Mountains.
Imagine tranquility. Imagine
sweat. Imagine.

Letter to Pearl

Kansas City, March 2008

Three months have passed since you went away. I've cried my eyes dry. Each time I look out through swollen eyelids, I ask God, why. Then I am reminded that you are rejoicing at your family reunion with Mother and Daddy. I smile.

I still dress "real fine" each day, whether I'm leaving home or not, whether I feel good or not when I wake up each morning. You often spoke about my dress in your own complimentary ways. "Merlee, I like your outfit. Where are you going today?" When I'd say, "Nowhere. Why?" You'd say, "You're looking "real fine." I thought you were going somewhere."

When you didn't speak of my dress, your eyes did. Like a road map, they started at my head
and meticulously traveled to my feet. You'd look away and begin to gently rock yourself back and forth. It began to happen often enough that I took notice, and finally made meaning of it. It was your warm, voiceless compliment.

I carry on the tradition the four of us girls had, capturing meaningful and humorous sayings from our lovely little community. Like, Miss Willie Jeff, our Sunday school teacher, who used to say, "I don't care whether I'm going somewhere or not. I don't care if I feel good or not. When I get up every morning, Willie Jeff is going to make herself look real fine." I am reminded each morning of her words as I get out of bed and make myself look "real fine."

Soon after you left, I spent three days in the hospital. My doctor's diagnosis was grief stress. During the days I spent there, I reflected on the happy times we had together and the challenges we had to endure, but we had each other.

After losing Mother and Daddy, we never grieved the way we should have grieved. I didn't know whether it was because we didn't know how to do so, or whether we adhered to society's tutorial: Hide your emotions, cry behind closed doors, take a few days off, and then resurface. Anyway, we got on with our life as best we could, as best we knew how. Today, I ask, "Who said?"

This time, I didn't emerge from grief in a few days. This time, I didn't adhere to society's grief tutorial. This time, someone greater than society captured my attention, and I listened. While I was hospitalized, waiting for my 2-gram sodium diet meals, potassium and antibiotic IVs, I was reminded of one of the most renown and effective steps program, Alcoholics Anonymous (AA). Initially used for alcoholics, research has proven it to be effective for non-alcoholics in various problematic areas. Step one: Admit you have a problem. Sister, I admitted that I had a problem. Mine was grief. My body heated up to a 103.8 temperature. My body cooled down to teeth chatters and body convulsions.

When I left the hospital, my doctor wrote a twelve-day script, unlike the lyrical twelve days of Christmas. Along with that, she ordered "Rest, rest and more rest." When I asked her how I could do that, especially with the semester starting in six days, she said, "Easy. You take a sabbatical or you take three daily doses of death." That convinced me.

I found a wonderful Grief Share ministry and have spent six rewarding weeks with other grievers like me. We have cried together, blown our nose together, and shared activities together. We made beautiful collages, each representing the favorite things our loved ones enjoyed. Cutting out of magazines reminded me of the times we cut out our favorite paper dolls. I chose beautiful pictures that represented your favorite thing to do, cook. Wondrous cooking. Scrumptious cooking. Blackberry cobblers and peach cobblers with mouth-watering flaky crusts, making chow-chow and your cornbread that even Aunt Jemima would love.

We wrote an essay about our loved one that captured memories, including the time we spent with them while they planned their departure from us. I was reminded of my anger about you leaving abruptly, not affording me the honor of being there with you as your journey came to a close. On the other hand, I could write about the precious memories, so I did and titled it "Home of a Lady Tiger." My narrative is packaged with laughter and highlights of your high school basketball days. I said you could pamper a meal far beyond the great cooks and great cookbooks. Your southern fried chicken and meat loaf could shut down a New Orleans kitchen. Your pastries could be the delight of France. Your laughter could scale the Colorado Mountains.

So, now, I write this letter and think of you. Good-bye is still inside the last jar of canned peach jelly you left on the top shelf of your pantry.

Silent Savor

The morning following Thanksgiving, Mimi is up at 6 a. m. I hear her bedroom door squeak open and shut; she keeps forgetting to put a drop of Bee Oil on the top hinge. I lay awake while she walks down the hallway and into the kitchen, her morning routine. It has been four months, but her belly still heaves every time she thinks of her first-born, dead at 42. I wonder what she'll eat this morning. I walk in and see her sitting at her table-for-two by the window, looking out on the lake, and eating a muddled meal of sliced beets on banana nut bread. I sit down and wait for the coffee to brew. She takes care not to leave anything on the plate, dragging each remaining crumb through juice the color of blood. I watch her carefully cull each breadcrumb into a miniature mass, making sure they get the red juice treatment before the last savor. Her heart hemorrhages. Our silence is humbling. I keep our silence company.

French Lace in Kansas City

Loose Park

Virgin white petals dabbed
with anemic yellow hues,
turned the corner. Chipmunk rested
in their shadow. Lifting two front legs
and clasping its two paws —prayer like.
After appearing to serve a quick, clumsy bow
to fragrant French Lace roses, Chipmunk
scurried across the sidewalk to explore
more varieties in the Rose Garden.
A light, south wind moved through the foliage,
stirred it to a nod —up, then down.
  A few stray mists from the fountain
  settled on my forehead.

Poems from
Under a Daylight Moon

Conversation with a Poem

Speak to me, Poem...I'm searching...for what no one
understands...
Are you doing time, Poem...a lot of poems do time...like
women
who inflict wrath on their no-good baby daddy...do no
good poems
desert their lovers...
Do no good poems ever apologize...no good poems get
confused...
because they are always looking to be found...like wanted
posters...
Have You Seen Me captions ...and blues guitars at
midnight...
looking for a poem to take home...
I know poems get rejected...like disco music in 1970s clubs
and the choir opening church service with Dry Bones...
people forget their origin... what helps them make it over...
what protects them...and what's on the other side of
through...
Share your plans, Poem...you can tell me...I hear you're a
hip-hop
artist... a film maker... working hard to earn recognition...
like a Grammy... you ever miss home...talk to me, Poem...
we'll discover what no one understands.

Survivor

— A Haiku

Sultry summer night.
A basketball smacks concrete.
He misses his friend.

December River

Late evenings in August
I sit in the backyard swing,
close my eyes, and pretend

I'm wearing a snow-crocheted camisole,
an icicle thong, and frosted sandals.

A drooping mimosa shades me.
Its blooms, like handmaids,
dab the sweat from my chest.

Sunrays paint a shimmering spot
on a cornflower blue backdrop.
Totally consumed in a state of musing,
I dive into December River.

Under a Daylight Moon

At noon, a woman plants lilies.
She hums.

The moon is pale,
the sunlight pristine,
an earthworm pushes
through a fresh mound
of black dirt.

The woman stops and inhales spring.
She hums, again.

Johnson Grass

After "Eel-Grass" by Edna St. Vincent Millay

Regardless of what I say
  All I really love to feel
Is the sun that brightens the day
  And the Johnson grass in the field
The clay dirt that waits for rain
  In spring and summer seasons
That creates tender grain
  And satisfies nature's reasons.

Barefoot Innocence

I walked barefoot with scorpions,
and played tag with black moccasins—
a twelve-year-old tomboy who climbed trees,

I dipped tadpoles from the bayou,
put them in gallon jars, and then
watched them turn into bullfrogs.

I picked wild berries by the quart,
polished my lips with the red ones,
and stored the rest in the bottom of fridge.

I dried sweat with berry-colored palms,
walked down to the bayou, sat on the bank,
and drowned my fussy feet in cold water.

I felt my first menses warm beneath me
and moved to a cooler spot of bluegrass.
Mosquitoes hummed haloes around my head.

The Four O'Clocks Whisper

Daddy died while on the outskirts of sleep
trapped between the smell of evening
                    and a changeless night.

Mother slept fleshless the rest of her life.

By day,
her dim eyes painted memories on every wall
in the house that Daddy built.
Voiceless prayers filled her nights.
Furious outbursts rested on her lips.
Four centuries of convention
planted in spring gardens, and flower beds
that only bloomed at four o'clock.
Now, the dust whispers from the earth.

Mother slept fleshless the rest of her life.

Make meaning of endings.
Follow them.

Good Night, Iris

Every day she cared for everybody in the house
and watched her favorite movie channel at noon.
Every morning she raised all the windows,
opened the screened doors, and shooed
away the lightning bugs.

She laughed at her diluted image in the bottom
of her favorite stainless steel pot just before
bubbles boiled her silhouette into vapors.
Saturday, she polished tile into sounds of a satin
orchestra, washed toilet bowls into Sunday morning,

and waxed hardwood floors that would be
the envy of Hattie McDaniel. And then,
at the end of every day,
her eyes hugged everyone good night,
and her irises tucked them into bed.

Saturday Anthem

For Grandmama and Grandpapa

Like going to church every Sunday,
I went to their house every Saturday morning.
I inhaled Grandmama's soul every time she said,
"Morning, Baby."

I could barely hear Billie Holiday singing
...Rich relations give...

The living room smelled like Friday night's smothered
Pheasant and month-old newspapers stacked on a
Chippendale chair that I never sat on.

Instead,

I made my way to my favorite velvet black chair
where I rested my hands on black satin arm covers.
Grandpapa sat in the kitchen across the hall
in his mahogany high chair forcing apple sauce oatmeal
through his cherry grape gums.

Them that's got shall get
Them that's not shall lose
So the Bible said and it still is news

He smiled.

Grandmama disappeared deep into the mansion
where she washed her hair highway black.
She returned with a huge white comb
protruding through the top of a white cone towel
carefully wrapped around her head.

Mama may have, Papa may have,
but God bless the child that's got his own.

Grandmama said it was blues for success.

Noah's Coffee House on the River

I want to get up one midnight before the moon yawns,
and stars pull the clouds over their heads,
before dew polishes the grass seductive green,
or frost plays heavy metal in the meadow.
I want to hear the first freighter horn
heave through cumulus clouds of fog.
I want to see the first sailboat interrupt dawn
as it rocks past an ancient oil freighter
barely piercing green water.
I want to be the first customer at Noah's Coffee House,
pour my first cup of scalding black coffee,
and find the first line of a new poem in the vapors.

Mother

I was your baby girl,
remember?
I remember nights in your bed
sleeping so hard that I hoped my breath
would heal my fallacies
and make meaning of Daddy's dreams

while too much grape Kool-Aid pees
on the soft sun-dried sheet beneath us.
You washed them in forgiveness
and hung them out to dry in pacific breezes
underneath a navel orange sun.

Sometimes I hear your smile,
smell your soul, and
hug your forgiveness tight.

In Reverse

I choose the booth overlooking the Plaza,
where the sun is piercing the window.
I order a hot pretzel and Oolong tea, and then
watch traffic crawling along the street below.
Groundskeepers pluck the last blooming plants
and bury summer in rich black dirt, but
the rosebushes remain untouched.

The letters in the store window across the street
are turned backward. Reminds me of the first time
my daughter met the alphabet. She frowned feverishly
as she pressed and pushed her pencil hard
between the lines of her pre-handwriting pattern paper.
The backward E's and S's made her happy.
Now, I smile as I look at the letters in reverse
and wonder if they make the storeowner happy.

A shopper standing in front of the window
resembles time staring at itself in the mirror.

Naked Blues

The piercing shrill from an ambulance
whines through the dingy morning light—
sifting her thoughts through shadows
of horror, which she wants to forget.
She rolls out of her sleeping bag, sits upright,
and wipes tired from her eyes.

Tears cover her brilliant auburn freckles
as she rolls the bag into a scroll
and fastens it to the harness on her back.
Once, she slept in the comfort of home.
The sting in her throat keeps the mad inside
as she shuffles memories into naked blues.

Girl Child

Flying far above the seasoned oak in the backyard,
two blue jays lament, and the December morning
embrace their echoes. Two mourning doves huddle
on the back porch side-by-side.

A nine-year-old girl child is sold into marriage.
She is divorced by age ten.
I wonder whether her father has any remorse.

If blue jays could talk,
they would give voice to the shame.
If mourning doves could cry,
they would grieve for the girl child.

Beethoven's Symphony No. 3
would call her, Eroica.

The Dead Pecker Bench

Every Saturday they sit on double benches
along the street that runs through town.
They spit their week through spaces where
teeth once stood in the seedtime of their lives.
They watch tight tails in blue jeans
swinging from side-to-side,
back and forth like the cadence of a two-stepper.
Irregular seams in their faces are buried storylines.
They wipe sweat from their temples and rest a hand
on the portal of their pants, while uneven language
falls off the edge of their seats. They capture curves
of swinging breasts and retrieve them at night
while the missus sleeps.

Fantasies in E Flat Major

Aged sun shines through crystal vases
and Eve draws Jack Daniels from a well.
Beethoven sits in a sailboat pantomiming
Symphony No. 5, and George Stevens reads
"The Greatest Story Ever Told" to dinosaurs
in Jurassic Park. Abraham grills a beast
in the shade of an olive tree while Sarah
suns on Queen Anne's lace.
The Red Sea is littered with water maples
waltzing to "The Art of Fugue."
I close my eyes and tuck my minor
fantasies in E flat major.

Drafting

The scent of coffee roams the kitchen searching for breakfast–
This morning I'm tired of my alien life
& my stuttering mind.

Today I'm moving to an ancient city
where I can smell the world again
& abandon the echoes of life's gall.

The first night,
I'll sleep beside the Dead Sea
& listen to the sound of peace.

Ten Tall Seasons and Then Some

for Manute Bol

Many times he was too tall
to walk through the average doorframe.
Most of the time he stood in the gap
to help his native Sudan. His smile
was as pure as ivory. His voice filled
Turalei, saturated Sudan, and reminded
the world of civil war in his homeland.
It was the rhapsody in his heart.
Imagine him lumbering through airports
and peering eyes climbing his frame
just to get a glimpse of the stars in his eyes.
Imagine seven feet of hockey on ice,
a seven-foot jockey riding horseback,
a seven-foot boxer in the ring, in the gym,
and in your face. Imagine him as Mother Teresa,
whose selflessness was endless, or Martin Luther
King, Jr., whose determination was ceaseless.
His NBA career can be seen in the eyes
of Sudanese school children. From Kansas to Sudan,
compassion and dignity traveled with him.

Draw a butterfly in the sky, and set it free.

Better Than Well

Professor hands their papers back.
It's the first one she's done
since high school senior English class
ten years ago. She tightens her lips,
inhales slowly, deeply, silently.

She turns to the last page of her paper,

gazes at the grade, and then, she
exhales slowly, carefully, silently.
She has done well. Better than well.
She relaxes her lips and lifts her head skyward.
For countless seconds, she smiles.

Poems from
It's Okay: Poetic Memoirs

Hush. Hear the Silence.

Silence is a giver, not a beggar.
It offers peace and comfort.
It doesn't attempt to out-talk anyone.
It doesn't even attempt to compete with anyone.
Silence never changes.
It is the same as yesterday.
It is the same today.
It will be the same tomorrow.
Let it shower you with peace
and blanket you with comfort.
Silence offers wisdom.
Hush.

The Storybook Heart

Open the cover and notice the author's name, yours.
Turn the page and note the copyright date, your birth.
Look further. You'll discover all your rights are reserved.
Read the table of contents, the chapters of your life.
Turn the page. Read the introduction, the preface of your life.
Turn another page and read a list of names, contributors
to the story of your life.

Humble yourself. Begin a lifetime.

Sun: Star of Summer

She belts out blistering temperatures
hotter than the latest dance craze moves.
Still, I don't want to stay inside.
I collect all my girlfriends
and head for my farm fave.
I take off my shoes
so pine needles can
pamper my feet
to a
treat.

She taunts farmlands and farm folks
with an audacious attitude kin
to bid whist artists and masters.
I collect all my girlfriends,
and head for the kitchen,
sweet tea on the rocks,
then back outside
to enjoy
pure parched
air.

Message in the Melody

I remember when
I was a ***wanna' be soprano***. I tried.
I remember when
I chose to be an ***alterin' alto***. I tried.
Now I am a ***strugglin' tenor.***
Still, I try.

Painting Images

Artists do it.
They paint winter landscapes, autumn scenes,
spring settings and summer sights.
Seizing a moment in time and place,
they capture the beauty they perceive
in images of people, places
and things of interest.
Simplicities and complexities.
They paint what they know.
They paint what they see.

Skeptics do it.
They use words to paint the environment
they perceive as a threat to their well-being.
Making meaning of their perceptions,
they paint stirring images of people,
places and things
that intimidate them.
Fears and doubts.
They paint what they don't know.
They paint what they don't see.

Wanting

Too many years
gone dormant,
too many days
fast asleep,
too much time
washed downstream.
Turbulent winters
frozen in place,
beautiful springs
silenced by haze,
aggressive summers
fermented in dampness,
tepid autumns
abandoned to images.
Wanting.

Spring Play

Winter had just lifted the weight of its arctic curtain, exposing a barren walnut tree
just outside the fence that divided the backyard from the field. Its giant trunk sat atop
the earth, sharing a piece of its brown and green space. While modeling an endless
waistline, it boasted bountiful muscled limbs. Some appeared to reach upward
as if grasping for the stars. Others appeared to sprawl outward. Certain that winter
company was gone, they began to dress. Mother Nature clothed them in tender green
leaves that would soon flirt with the sun. And then, she dabbed them with fragrant buds
that would blossom in the arms of quiet breezes. Virgin, carefree blooms stared tenderly
into the eyes of soft breezes. Warmed by day and cooled by night, they begged the moments
to never end. Nature's vigilant eyes witnessed the annual spring play staged by winter's flight.
A barren walnut tree, limbs, leaves, buds, blossoms and soft breezes; a love story.

Soon, a birth. Walnuts.

Petals

Eyes behold their appearance
while minds study their shape
and spirits admire their grace.
They wave from the kiss of a breeze,
cradle the dews of a spring morning,
and are caressed by raindrops after a shower.
They sun in the still of a summer day,
offer comfort to insects that come to visit,
befriend butterflies that take rest from flight
or come to take pleasure in their pollen.
They appear to be committed to their season
and patient with their visitors.
They accept a brief, fragile life of serenity
and humility until their passing.

Nature Matters

A blade of grass
A bug on a blade of grass
A leaf on a tree
A bug on a leaf on a tree
A flower petal
A bug on the flower petal
Gently it rests
On the blade of grass
Gently it crawls
About the leaf on the tree
Gently it explores
The back of the flower petal
Grass
A leaf
A bug
A tree
A flower petal
Nature matters.

Clippings

Her heart is her personal library
where she lets her thoughts browse
its many shelves. Her eyes stare
softly into yesterday. She remembers.
Unlike clock alarms set for a certain
waking hour, her alarms are unannounced.

She imagines morning when the house
was filled with prodigal breakfast
aromas taunting nostrils and daring
anyone to sleep late.

She remembers open trails
zigzagging through the farm
and cool wooded areas. Each
one etched with care; tall grass
and briar branches pushed aside,
signs of frequent visitors.

Her eyes often stare into yesterday
and a trail of thoughts tickle her memories.

Unconditional Grounds

The grounds around the house were always friendly.
They were vulnerable to all the seasonal elements.
Spring rains played hide and seek with the new grasses.
Summer storms taunted the flower and vegetable gardens.
Autumn temperatures frolicked carelessly on veteran soils.
Winter air challenged the dusty, gravel trails to
games of scrimmage.
The grounds around the house were always friendly,
giving much and receiving all.

Mud Pies

Mornings arrived early with quiet daybreak songs.
Their gentle notes touched one eyelid, then the other.
Wakefulness stirred all five of my senses, while
the presence of unrelenting dawns reminded me
"Rise now, your playhouse awaits you."
In the midst of the early summer mornings,
my growing bare feet carried me to the backdoor
of the kitchen where I gazed upon a sleepy backyard
and a yet slumbering field, a welcoming audience.
In the silence of the early summer mornings,
while a lazy sun had breakfast with a yawning horizon,
I made mud pies in my playhouse.

Literacy in the Barnyard

We sat on the floor in the door of the barn.
Daddy's feet rested on the ground,
mine dangled loosely beside his ankle.
I was eager for the day they would rest
flat on the ground beside his.
Outside the gate, Tansy, the milk cow,
and Daisy, the plow horse, were enjoying
hay and grains. Daddy's gaze at them was one
of a contented father.

I picked up the book I had brought with me,
A Child's Primer, with colorful short narratives
about Baby Ray and Little Boy Blue.
I opened it and said, "Daddy, let's read."
The gentle movement of his head in my direction
was his silent confirmation, "Okay."
We began our lesson, me pointing and gliding
my right index finger underneath each word.
Gulps of air preceded his efforts to call words.
We sat on the floor in the door of the barn
each animal quietly listening while we read.

Breakfast Delights

The crack of dawn found her tickling
the bellies of her floured biscuit dough.
Like the certainty of daybreak,
she prepared them every morning,
carefully mixing her memorized recipe,
then fluffing them into their just right shapes.
Mother placed each mass of dough
on her favorite baking pan.
With a look of contentment,
she opened the oven door,
placed them on the rack,
and trusted a sizzling temperature
to transform them into healthy
flaky brown, breakfast delights.

Salvaged Comforts and a Sister's Stories

a humorous birthday tribute to Pearl Lee (Booster)

Teddy Bear and Dolly sprawled comfortably on a bed made with care. They didn't seem to mind keeping company with the myriad of shapes and designs representing the pride of one family's clothing lineage. So, they rested peacefully while one of Mother's handmade quilts whispered
colorful tales about the nature of its characters. Each salvaged scrap of fabric shared amusing tales about their wear to school, to work, to church and to play. Teddy Bear and Dolly appeared amused by the rhapsody of the stories, but somberly removed by the quiet strength and courage that emerged from each one of them. Each pair of faded pupils stared in the distance while kindred spirits continued their tireless journey in the attitude of warm service.

Today, one of those kindred spirits continues her journey. Fabric once adorned by her can still be seen in handmade quilts from long ago. Now and again, she revisits the sojourns of her life.
Once in a while, she shares a choice chapter from her narratives. Observe as she thoughtfully recreates humorous dramas. Listen carefully as she cleverly plants the storyline inside the plot.
Pay close attention while she creates colorful characters by using meticulous details sure to awaken the imagination. There are Mother and Daddy stories, Joe, Jr., Pearl Lene and Cleter Bell stories.

There are Merlee stories and even her own Booster stories. For example, there is Butlah, The Great Cucumber Picker and her Basketball Adventures on the Rocks. There are the infamous Miss Willie's Sunday School stories, not to mention her acting debut in the high school play, "The Devil's Funeral." Like Teddy Bear and Dolly, watch and listen as a remarkable storyteller and a natural actress bring the theater of your mind to life. Ask a living kindred spirit, who has the memory of a griot, to share some amusing tales from her memoirs of salvaged comforts.

She smiles. Then grins. The stories begin.

A Christmas Chronicle

Every Christmas four little girls followed their daddy into the woods of their farm in search of the perfect evergreen to cut down, bring home and decorate. One that breathed aromatic cedar fragrances which penetrated the living room and beyond reminding the family of the true reason to celebrate Christmas. One that proudly stood while they added ornaments and Christmas lights. Preparation for the season was a pure family affair, both in spirit and in deed. The day was planned and the activities began. The girls decorated the tree, and their mother did what she absolutely loved, holiday baking —goodies for family, friends and uninvited guests. Each one dashed with special love from her best kept secret recipes. Daddy minded the fire and relaxed in front of it in his favorite chair. He watched the girls decorate their perfect Christmas tree, while enchanting aromas from the kitchen pierced his nostrils and the love of his family soothed his tired soul.

He Made the Universe

He made the universe.
Fishes giggling about life
in the rivers, the oceans and the seas;
fowl risking flight through
the atmosphere that surrounds them;
animals daring to move freely within their means;
plant life tickling the earth's soil with its growth.
They are symbols of the cost of freedom
that comes when total trust
is put into action.
Like the fishes, let's giggle
about life in the universe.
Like the fowl, let's risk
our dreams by taking flight.
Like the animals, let's dare
to move freely, but with purpose.
Like the plant life, let's humor Him
by tickling our faith.
For, He made the universe.

Closing New Poems

I Owe You a Song

An Ekphrastic Poem, after the painting "The Blood in the Veins," by Rachel Slotnick

We delight in the beauty of the butterfly, but rarely admit the changes it has gone through to achieve that beauty.
– Maya Angelou

I am an offspring of a broken history where journeys ended
without ending and tears survived as long as life breathed.
I am
an offspring of the rhythm of courage, symphony of strength,
psalm of wisdom, harmony of hope and the exodus of change.
Severe sunlight streaming from a spacious blue sky, you
agonized in dense harvests, your fleeting breaths tip-toeing
between pitiless plantation rows glaring like endless.

I wish you could see the beautiful you never saw. I wish you
could see the view from Pike's Peak, rest in orchard shade
of apple and cherry trees, walk through rows of amber grain
and inhale America. I am an offspring of women, who wore
their hats like a silent anthem introducing every Sunday
service. Eyes reverently awed the brilliant art of each crown
sharing a historical lyric of triumph and esteem.

I can hear your muted beauty in my hat of many flowers.

Three Postcard Poems

It's your birthday, but I gift
myself a memory of us, two
main ideas, an evening when
silence consoled our stroll
along the seashore. We were
hungry for lyrics of again and
thirsty for a toast to revive them.
O, how I miss us.

It's your birthday, but I gift
myself a memory of us, two
main ideas, on a freezing night
by a cozy fireside. We adored
with delight the sight and sound
of chanting flames dancing
with the resolve of ballet artists.
O, how I miss us!

Absence is present every day,
like the student I can't remember.
Every day, hope is present and precise
counteracting the gravity of grief,
dissolving moments and distilling
a state of being. We were barefoot
survivors seeing inside each other's
armor. It was not an act.
O, how I miss us!

Mahalia Jackson and Lady

for Mother

From a distance, I watch the serene face of Lady pause in mid-morning, rest both elbows on the kitchen sink, and stare out the window as far as her pair of eyes allow her to travel the outskirts of a titanic, pampered farm. She pauses her day list to spend some time with her favorite gospel artist and friend to her dreams.

Lady waits momentarily with a not quite smile while the piano introduces her friend. I turn the volume up on each one of my ears. Lady and her favorite gospel artist enter " The Upper Room." I watch the not quite smile soften into a genuine full smile. Like someone from a far terrain arriving with an apology and a promise.

I can only imagine what each woman has in mind, but I do know what they have in common, a Black woman living in America unfolding their brain and unraveling their tongue to practice words that sweat behind silent stories. The plot, their sobering spirituality inside their museum of presence.

Birthing Exodus

an Ekphrastic Poem

An air of serenity liberates my body, like unwinding morning glories
to help me find voice so I can pen notable narratives of who I am.

My passion is like the first woman giving birth to humanity, who
launched bloodlines that still ripple like waterways through maps.

My love is steeped in the soul of ancient romance, persevering
and immovable as the mystifying prehistoric Stonehenge.

My patience is as novel as the offerings of the Mother Road
that takes care of trippers during the trek of their travels.

Serenity is the exodus that walks close to me, so close to me
that I can smell the smiles on the other side of through.

I move forward seated while gazing into a consonance of silence,
memorizing faces like phrases, prayers and the humming of summer.

Humanitarian: An Arc

You breathe light into the branches of souls.
You are a bright promise fulfilling diverse goals.

You reach across the world like an arc.
You give happy a color inside night hearts
searching for honorable examples of guidance.
You foster human well-being, a pillar of reliance.

You shoulder shadowed dreams inside silent sands
of lullabies sealed in subtle moonlit dreamlands.
You are a song, distant laughter, an ode to humanity
Like the solitude of moon an influence of earth sanity

You breathe light into the branches of souls.
You are a bright promise fulfilling diverse goals.

A Peace Symphony

I want the world to breathe
like mornings yawning awake,
sit quietly like the beautiful lotus
and rest as still as fog,
like dew collecting on a spider web,
like soil slowly evaporating water,
like moisture evaporating from leaves.
I want the world to abandon
the demanding mental interstate,
walk among slash pines and listen
to them speak softly to a breeze,
inhale a fragrant flower forest,
caress a fallen bloom and
adore the harmony of diversity.
I want the world to pause restless thoughts,
release them one by one, breathe kindly
and listen to a symphony of peace.

Pass the smiles, please.

MARY ROGERS-GRANTHAM is an Arkansas native, award winning poet, and a college professor. She adores family and teaching, respects nature and humanity, and enjoys writing and exploring. This collection, *Shifting Shades of Sunlight: New and Selected Poetry and Prose,* includes new poetry and poems from earlier publications. She is working on her next poetry collection *A Rainbow at Midnight.*

www.ingramcontent.com/pod-product-compliance
Lightning Source LLC
LaVergne TN
LVHW091118150826
845673LV00002B/887

* 9 7 9 8 9 8 7 3 1 8 4 2 3 *